WINNING WEB SITES

WINNING WEB SITES

HOW TO IDENTIFY YOUR IDEAL CLIENTS ... AND SELL MORE TO THEM!

Alison Silbert

iUniverse, Inc.

New York Lincoln Shanghai

WINNING WEB SITES
HOW TO IDENTIFY YOUR IDEAL CLIENTS … AND SELL MORE TO THEM!

iUniverse books may be ordered through booksellers or by contacting:

iUniverse
2021 Pine Lake Road, Suite 100
Lincoln, NE 68512
www.iuniverse.com
1-800-Authors (1-800-288-4677)

Because of the dynamic nature of the Internet, any Web addresses or links contained in this book may have changed since publication and may no longer be valid.

The views expressed in this work are solely those of the author and do not necessarily reflect the views of the publisher, and the publisher hereby disclaims any responsibility for them.

ISBN: 978-0-595-47089-1 (pbk)

ISBN: 978-0-595-91371-8 (ebk)

Printed in the United States of America

CONTENTS

PART III: CONNECTING YOUR IDEAL VISITOR WITH YOUR WEBSITE

Preface

Who should read this book?

This book is ideal for anyone who

- spends valuable time and money telling people their website exists

- feels they are not visible in the search engine listings

- gets visitors coming to the website, but doesn't get enough business through the website

- owns and operates a small business and wants to develop a website presence to boost sales and customer awareness

- wants to develop a website for reasons other than a business

What you will learn from reading this book

This book teaches you how to create an effective website. An effective website is one that *compels people to do what you want them to do*. For example, if you operate a business and have a website that people can visit and use to buy your products, then an effective website needs to be more than a simple product catalog identifying the features and qualities that make your products unique. An effective website will also tell your customers why they need to buy your products and how your products will improve their lives. Moreover, it has to leave visitors wondering how they ever survived without your products. At the same time, it has to be visible to all your prospective clients; easy to find, easy to read and easy to remember.

How to read this book

This book is divided into three distinct parts.

The first part talks about the purpose of having a website. Sounds crazy, right? Why would you need to learn about why you want this website? The reason is simple. Once you have a crystal clear understanding of who your audience is (we call this your 'ideal visitor') and what they think and feel, you are in a better position to sell them what they need (the whole reason they come to your website in the first place!)

The second part of this book tells you how to put together a website that your ideal visitor feels they **have to** buy from. A website that tells them to buy now or else they risk losing a chance for something so valuable to them their life will never be the same again.

The third part of this book tells you how to tell the world that your website exists. It goes into detail about what is involved in putting your website 'online' where the world can see it from home or work on their own computers. It then goes into helpful hints of how to move up the ladder in the world of search engines (Google, Yahoo, etc.). Ideally, whenever someone initiates a search on the internet, you want your website to be found at the top of the first page of search results. If someone runs a search and gets thousands or even millions of results, they are not going to review them all. For many, only the first page of results gets any attention at all.

Acknowledgments

Mark Biciunas—Agorex—for the idea of writing this book

Jennifer Beale—Unleash PR—for helping me stay on track when I veer off…

Editor

Illustrator

Family—for being there when I need you!

PART I

▼

WHY DO I WANT A WEBSITE?

This is a question that will probably have several answers. For each individual or business, the answers will be different. Some might provide extremely basic answers, such as "to increase sales" or "to market my products and services to a wider audience". Others might provide a more specific answer, such as "to establish an e-commerce system whereby my existing customers can order and pay for their products and services on-line, thereby reducing my costs and keeping my retail prices competitive".

As you can see from these simple illustrations, there are many different reasons for having websites. A more important question to ask yourself may be "Why would I **NOT** want a website?" or even "What is the cost to me of not having a website?"

A website is the premier sales and marketing tool of the 21st century. Just as people would go to a store and browse in the 1950's, or visit a shopping mall in the 1980's, the customer of today browses on the internet. This is how many people find businesses that are selling the products and services they require. This is an important, but often overlooked concept. A website does not help you find customers … it helps customers find YOU!

Think of your website as a different kind of store-front. If people are browsing, or window-shopping, you would want to have a store front where they can see it. Equally importantly, though, how would you design your store-front in order to entice the right kind of shopper to come inside?

CHAPTER 1

▼

WHO IS MY IDEAL
VISITOR?

What you will learn in this chapter:

1. What an ideal visitor is

2. How to determine your ideal visitor

3. Why you need to **know** your ideal visitor

What is an ideal visitor?

The concept of an ideal visitor seems simple on the surface. Ideal. Best. Who is the best person to visit my website? Simple enough, but exploring a little deeper you start to wonder. Just who **is** the best person to have visiting my website, and more importantly, **what makes them the best**?

Imagine ...

Think back to when you were a child. It's the beginning of summer. You are young and full of energy, the only care you have is who you were playing with that Saturday, or whether your favorite team was going to make the playoffs. Remember days when the ice cream truck came rolling down the street? What did you do? I know I used to run to my mother saying "Ice Cream! Ice Cream! Mom, can I have an ice cream??" Who do you think the ice cream trucks came into the neighborhood for: the busy parents or the rambunctious children, begging their parents for an ice cream?

The answer is clear: everything about the ice cream truck, from the brightly painted pictures on the front and sides to the music that they played to the person driving it was aimed at the children. Chances are the music drove your parents crazy—but to you it was the most wonderful sound in all the world.

Now take that rambunctious child wanting ice cream, and put that concept into your business. What would that look like for you? What would happen to your productivity? What would happen to your income? Would the operations or staffing of your business change, and if so, how? Who would your ideal customers be, and how would you recognize them? What would you give to your ideal customers? What would they give back to you?

I can't answer those questions for you. I can tell you my version of an ideal customer, however. In an ideal world, my business would be filled with people who enjoy helping others, people who put others' needs before their own. The clients are completely satisfied with their product and service levels. Whenever a customer has a concern, it is voiced constructively, responded to promptly, and resolved to everyone's satisfaction. My ideal client would know who they want to reach via the Internet and what they want to tell those people.

What does your ideal client look like? How do you know you are reaching them? How do your results change when you are helping an ideal client?

Ideal Visitor
A person looking at your website that fits all of your pre-determined requirements. For example, an ideal visitor for a baby clothes store website would be a new parent or grandparent looking for baby clothes.

How do I know who my ideal visitor is?

Following along the previous analogy that the internet is the store-front of the 21st Century, the ideal visitor to your website is the same as the ideal store shopper who would visit your retail store, if you have one.

Let's narrow down this concept of an ideal client focusing on one marketing tool: the Internet. Every website has visitors, right? Using the concept of your ideal client, you can now identify characteristics that identify the ideal visitor to your website:

- What do they like? What do they dislike?
- What are their hobbies and interests?
- What is important to them?
- What phase of life are they in (childhood, adolescence, early adulthood, child-rearing, mid-life, retired)?
- What is their marital status?
- What are their fundamental societal and religious beliefs?
- Where do they live?

These are just a few sample considerations. All of these questions are important considerations and should be taken into account when you set out to create a website. This applies equally to a brand new website, to a redesign or overhaul of an existing website, or to the addition of new content (sub-pages) to your current website.

Below is a sample demographics form to get you thinking about your ideal visitor, and what that looks like for you and your website. Take a look through it, and start answering some of the questions.

Demographics Form:

Use the table below to write in the demographics for your ideal visitor.

Location (country, state, city, etc.)	
Age (child, youth, early adulthood, child-rearing, senior, etc.)	
Education (high school, college, University, etc.)	

Income (high, medium, low, $ amount)	
Net Worth (assets minus liabilities)	
Occupation & Position (CEO, manager, secretary, computers, school, etc.)	
Personal Characteristics (marital status, beliefs—religious or otherwise)	

Again, this is just a sample table. You can freely add or modify fields in this form to tailor the form around your business, your products and services, and most importantly, **your ideal visitor**. If your ideal visitor can be clearly segmented or identified purely on a basis of their favourite brand of chip dip, then put such a field into your demographics form, as well as their favourite brand of chips, the amount of money they spend on chips, etc.

You see the point. Tailor the form to meet your needs.

Why do I need to know who my ideal visitor is?

There are many reasons you should know who your ideal visitor is. In this section, I will go over a few of these reasons. The following is a short list of some of the reasons:

1. Visitors will know right away if they can use your product or service.

2. You can write in a style suited for your ideal visitor.

3. You will know who you can service and who needs to go elsewhere.

Let's use an example to examine these reasons in a little more detail. Let's say you are selling cowboy hats from a store in western Canada. Would you expect your customers to be men or women? What age would most of your customers be (children, teens, new mothers, middle-aged women, seniors)? Would you need your customers to have a certain amount of money available to them for surplus spending?

Likely Customers Characteristics

- Gender: Males and females

- Location: within 20 miles of the store

- Age: any age with the authority to spend money

- Education: N/A

- Income Level: enough to spend a little on 'extras' or 'amusement'

- Net Worth: N/A

- Work/Job title: N/A

- Personal Status: N/A

- Hobbies/Interests: cowboys, riding, ranch, western

Would you try to sell a cowboy hat to a beggar on the street? No. Why not? You probably have a pretty good idea that they don't have the money to spend on cowboy hats. Similarly, would you try to sell a suit to a farmer? Probably not. Why? Because the farmer spends most of his time outdoors working, and has little or no need for a dress suit. A farmer probably only keeps one suit for special occasions. A professional person, on the other hand, probably wears a different suit every day for work.

If you know the farmer won't wear a suit, and a beggar probably won't buy a hat, then why create one set of marketing materials geared for everyone? You are wasting your own time and resources to market towards a customer that cannot or will not buy your products and services. Similarly, your ideal customer viewing the website will see that you sell to everyone, and may be turned off.

Define Your Ideal Visitor

Take some time now and write down all the characteristics of your ideal visitor. You can make up your own demographics form or download the sample demographics form from www.idealvisitor.com.

Chapter Overview

In this chapter you learned:

1. what an ideal visitor is

2. how to identify your ideal visitor

3. why it is important to identify your ideal visitor

Coming Up ...

In the next chapter you will learn how to see the real message your ideal visitor is receiving (not necessarily what you think you are saying), what your ideal visitor wants to know, and how to tell your ideal visitor what he wants to know.

CHAPTER 2

▼

WHAT DOES MY IDEAL VISITOR WANT TO KNOW?

What you will learn in this chapter:

1. how to see the message your ideal visitor is receiving

2. what your ideal visitor wants to know

3. how to tell your ideal visitor what he wants to know

4. why you need to understand what your ideal visitor sees

"Don't criticize what you don't understand, son.
You never walked in that man's shoes"

—*Elvis Presley*

How do I See the Message my Ideal Visitor is Receiving?

Imagine ...

You arrive at work, and your colleague is sitting at your desk, doing your work. You ask her why she is doing this. She responds "the boss has decided to mix the jobs around for a day, and I'm doing yours. You get to do Sharon's job today."

Sharon is the boss.

What is your immediate reaction? Fear? Anxiety? Excitement? Amusement?

Suddenly you find yourself forced to step into your boss' shoes.

Stepping into another person's shoes—your ideal visitor's—is what you need to do so that you can see what your ideal visitor sees when he comes to your website. How? Be creative. Draw on your existing knowledge of your ideal visitor. Is your ideal visitor male or female? What does your ideal visitor do in a day? Where does he live and work? Why is your ideal visitor coming to you? What problem does he have that you can solve?

Once you have answered these questions about your ideal visitor, look at your website from his eyes. What messages are you getting? What part of the website is important to you? Does the website ask you to do anything, and if so, what are you asked to do? (e.g. Make a phone call, order a product, look at another web page, sign up for a newsletter, etc.)

Take some time to review your existing website, while trying to take on the perspective of your ideal visitor. Think about the messages you are receiving and whether the content is clear and easily understandable.

Some things you might want to consider are the language used in your website. Is it free from jargon or terms that are second nature to you but might be completely unintelligible to a prospective customer? Does it use abbreviations (which might be equally difficult for a customer to understand)?

What Does my Ideal Visitor Want to Know?

So far, you have defined your ideal visitor, and looked at your website from their perspective. Now you are ready to discover what your ideal visitor wants to learn from your website.

The first step on this road to discovery is an analysis of yourself.

What you want to know

When you want to know something, what are you looking for?

- An answer to a question
- A solution to a problem
- something else

Where do you look for the answers?

- A resource center (books, tapes, CDs, videos, DVDs)
- A trusted person (friend, colleague, teacher, family member)
- The Internet
- somewhere else

Why do you choose this resource?

- It's easy (to find, to use, etc.)
- You trust it/believe in it
- The level of risk it involves is within your comfort zone
- some other reason

What your ideal visitor wants to know

Take the answers from the questions above and store them for a minute. Get back into the mindset of your ideal visitor: what that person looks like, feels like, acts like; consider what is important to him or her.

Once you are in the mindset of your ideal visitor, ask yourself these questions again:

- When you want to know something, what are you looking for?
- Where do you look for the answers?
- Why do you choose this resource?

Pick up the page with the answers to the first questions. Now write down the answers to the same questions, using your ideal visitor's view point.

What did you discover? Did you discover why your ideal visitor would come to you over-and-above your competition?

The similarities and differences

Take the two sets of answers you created, and put them side by side. How are they similar? How are they different? What led to the similarities and differences in the answer sets?

A practical example

Scenario: you are sitting at your desk and you need to find a book publisher. You open Internet Explorer, go to Google, and type in 'book publisher'. A second or two later, a list of thousands of websites appears. You start scanning the first page of the list.

What catches your eye and makes you want to click on a particular link?

When I use Google to look for a website and get over 50 results, I start scanning the first few links for '*keywords*'.

Keyword

A word that is used to find a website on a specific topic. For example, to find a website on photography, keywords could be "photo", "photography", "picture", "colour" or "black and white".

Another example is taken from Brian Klemmer's book "If how-to's were enough, we would all be skinny, rich and happy" (paraphrased):

The class facilitator tells the students to open their book to a blank page and take out a pen. The facilitator then tells the students to "Write your name with your non-writing hand as many times as possible". This required the right-handed students to start writing with their left hand, and vice-versa. The students are given a set amount of time. When there is only 10 seconds left, the facilitator repeatedly tells the students to "hurry up, you're running out of time", and provides them with a ten-second count down.

When the exercise is complete, students are asked to share what they felt during the exercise (e.g. did they feel they had to write a certain way? Did they feel pressured or relaxed by the time limitation?)

The point of this example is simple—it is not easy to do something a different way when you have been doing it the same way your whole life. Putting yourself into the position of trying to think like someone else is not easy.

When I was a child, every summer I would lie on the lawn in the back yard and gaze up at the sky. It didn't matter what color the clouds were, I would consistently find some kind of shapes (animals, geometric shapes, people's heads, etc.) and point them out to whoever I was with at the time (parents, friends, etc.) As time wore on, I lost that child-like creativity. It became harder and harder to think like a carefree child without having the prejudices and biases of an adult creeping into the picture. Eventually, clouds became nothing more than clouds."

How to Figure out What your Ideal Visitor Wants to Know

There are many ways to figure out what your ideal visitor wants to know. The simplest way to do this is to imagine yourself in his or her position. What problems is your ideal client facing? What help does he or she need? Why would your ideal client go looking for your product or service? Why would he or she buy your product or service over your competition?

Take a moment now to answer these questions on a sheet of paper.

Again, a practical example illustrates the point. If you are a supplier of industrial cookware, then your ideal client would be the owners of large restaurants. To put yourself fully into their position, you need to imagine yourself as the owner of a restaurant.

What problems are you facing? You could be dealing with staffing problems, either a shortage of people, or conflicts between people. Your objective is to fill your restaurant with happy repeat customers and keep your profits high. What problems or issues might be preventing that from happening? Quality concerns, menu issues, difficulties with the kitchen staff and a host of other possibilities come to mind. A kitchen supplier would not be able to help with many of these, but focus on the ones you could assist with. If there is a problem with food preparation, then new kitchen equipment is a possible solution.

What help do you need? If you have identified that kitchen equipment is a possible solution to a problem, then the help you need is to find the right kitchen equipment to suit your menu and the size of your facility at a reasonable price.

If you already have an existing relationship with one supplier, then chances are that they will be the first person you call, but for a large expenditure, you would probably want to shop around. What elements are you looking for? Price? Installation and downtime? After-market service? Reputation? There are many possibilities.

Come back to yourself now and determine how you can satisfy these requirements not just for one customer but for many.

Why do I need to understand what my Ideal Visitor Sees?

First of all, you need to understand what your ideal visitor sees because you want to connect with him or her. You want your ideal visitor to feel an emotional connection, to say to himself or herself "Wow, this person really understands what I'm going through."

The ability to connect with your ideal client means that you have a higher chance of convincing him or her to buy your product or service. You can connect with your ideal client in a few ways:

- evoke emotion using words
- evoke emotion using pictures
- create a feeling of urgency

To evoke emotion using words, you can use phrases like "Call now! This offer will expire in only 10 days!" or "This is an offer of a lifetime!" The danger with some of these terms, however, is that they are over-used, and everyone is exposed to them all the time. As such, their effectiveness starts to diminish somewhat. The key is to find words that will work for your ideal client.

To evoke emotion using pictures, think of things that you love or hate. Find pictures that create these strong emotions, and include them in your website. Again, you have to tailor this to the mindset of your ideal client. Most people have a strong emotional response to pictures of puppies or kittens, but they aren't going to help you sell restaurant equipment.

Words and pictures can both help to create a feeling of urgency. When you are building a website, remember also that words and pictures are pretty much all you have to work with. While some websites do contain audio files as well, many people tend to turn the sound down or off, and jump away from noisy websites.

Continuing with the example of the supplier of industrial kitchen equipment, there are many ways to create emotion and a feeling of urgency that might apply. You could make use of images of dingy, dilapidated kitchens and contrast them with pictures of pristine, white kitchens with brand new, modern equipment. You could use words that ask "Are you losing customers because it takes too long for the food to get to the table?" More directly, you could say "Upgrade your kitchen today, and stop losing customers tomorrow!" The choice of images and words is ultimately up to you, but they must always be evaluated from the perspective of your ideal client.

How do I Tell my Ideal Visitor What He Wants to Know?

Once you have determined what your ideal visitor wants to know, you are ready to start your story. Shown below is a sample chart you can fill out to help you write your website content. You can also find this chart on the Ideal Visitor website: *www.idealvisitor.com*.

Writing for Your Ideal Visitor	
Unique Value Proposition **What makes you different?**	

Writing for Your Ideal Visitor	
Supporting Message #1	
Supporting Message #2	
Supporting Message #3	
Supporting Message #4	

Once you have filled out the chart, you can take your notes and start expanding them into sentences and paragraphs. Remember to write from the perspective of your ideal visitor.

Ultimately, you may have multiple unique value propositions, but it is best to focus as much as you can. Don't try to be all things to all people. Focus on your ideal visitor, his or her needs, and you will bring yourself success. Concluding the example of the industrial kitchen equipment supplier, your unique value proposition might be that you can save your clients some money. Supporting messages might include:

1. An extensive catalog of all the best products
2. Competitive prices
3. Professional installation
4. Extended warranties and after-market service & support
5. Experienced salespeople who can ensure that your customers get the right product for their kitchen
6. Refund/Return policy
7. References and testimonials from satisfied customers
8. Statistics
   a. How many of your customers are repeat customers
   b. How long have you been in business

    c.   Do you supply or service any major chains

    d.   Do any celebrity chefs use your products in their restaurants

9.   Additional services you can provide. For example, would you have your salespeople visit a prospective client and evaluate their needs or simply take an order?

Chapter Overview

In this chapter you have learned how to:

1.   see the message your ideal visitor is receiving

2.   identify what your ideal visitor wants to know

3.   tell your ideal visitor what he wants to know

Coming Up …

In the next chapter you will learn how to recognize what your ideal visitor wants to do on your website.

CHAPTER 3

▼

WHAT DOES MY IDEAL VISITOR WANT TO DO ON MY WEBSITE?

What you will learn in this chapter:

1. how to determine what your ideal visitor wants to do on your website
2. what primary and secondary calls to action are
3. how to create a strong call to action

How do I know what my Ideal Visitor wants to do on my website?

To figure out what your ideal visitor wants to do on your website, put yourself in his or her shoes and ask yourself "why would I want to come to this website?" Here are some ideas of why people would come to a website:

- to learn about your topic or to take a course
- to buy a product/service

- to sell something

Depending on your purpose for building a website, you could easily have to accommodate all of these needs and more. A business that retails nutritional supplements might have identified their ideal client as someone who is concerned about their own health or that of a family member. Why would such a person visit their website?

The ideal client may be concerned, but not knowledgeable on the subject of nutrition. For that reason, they may come to the website looking for information before jumping to the conclusion that they need to purchase something. As a retailer, you might add pages onto your website that deal with the different nutrient levels in different foods, with physical fitness and activity levels, or with the warning signs of serious problems and conditions associated with lack of nutrition. Perhaps you could build a short quiz or test into the website, making it interactive. The ideal visitor could spend two minutes answering questions, and the test results could then shock them into becoming a customer.

An important thing in all circumstances is to make the website easy to use. If you want people to purchase items from you directly through the website, then you need more than just a catalog of your inventory and prices. You need a system to accept payment by credit cards or via *Paypal* and to keep an up-to-date database of your e-commerce sales so that you can follow up. If someone buys nutritional supplements, you may want to automatically send them an e-mail when their supply is starting to run low.

What is a Call to Action?

A call to action answers the question "that's interesting … how do I get your product or service?" Whatever it is that you want your user to do, ***tell him!*** One of the most common mistakes made when creating a website is the failure to use a call to action. Why would your ideal visitor buy your product or service if you don't ask them to?

Another way to look at this concept is to contrast an in-person sale with an internet sale. The call to action is the closing pitch.

What is a Primary Call to Action?

A primary call to action is the most important thing you want your ideal visitor to do. Do you want him/her to:

1.   Call you for more information?

2.   Visit your retail facility/warehouse?

3.   Buy your products directly from the website?

4.   Look at more material on your website?

5.   Respond to an active discussion?

For example, if you are selling nutritional supplements on a website, you want your ideal visitor to buy one or more different supplements, right? So ***ask them!*** Seems simple, right? It is. However, so many people create their marketing materials (brochures, business cards, flyers, website, etc.) with no sense of urgency and no call to action. What would you do if you came across a website that has exactly what you are looking for, but no way to purchase it? You would probably research the item, and then go someplace else to purchase it. **This means your website would actually be working to the benefit of your competitors!** Why would you put out marketing pieces that lack a crucial element? Convincing someone to buy is how you close the deal. Now your visitor is no longer just an ideal client, they are a paying customer.

What is a Secondary Call to Action?

A secondary call to action is what you want your ideal visitor to do if he or she is not comfortable carrying out your primary call to action. For example, if your primary call to action asks your ideal visitor to purchase nutritional supplements, then your secondary call to action may be something like

"If you prefer, come into our retail offices where one of our trained nutritionists would be happy to consult with you to ensure that you are getting the best possible product for your family!"

Why do I need a strong call to action?

There are many reasons you need a strong call to action in your marketing materials. This text covers a few of the more important reasons to create strong calls to action.

Some of the reasons you need a strong call to action are:

1. to turn prospects into clients

2. to create a sense of urgency

3. to shorten the time lapse between prospecting and closing the sale

4. to convince existing customers to buy more of your product/service

These four reasons are all significant and worthy of a little more detail.

Reason 1: To turn prospects into clients

This reason should be fairly self-explanatory. Who does **not** want to create clients from prospects? Everybody I know that is doing business today wants more business.

Once you have provided your prospect with all the information necessary to show him or her that they need your products or services, you tell them to buy now. Use language that is strong enough that they don't want to leave the website without placing an order right then and there.

Remember the point that was made a couple of pages back. If you don't close the sale, then the prospect is likely to have researched the product on your website only to buy it someplace else. Again, **this means your website would actually be working to the benefit of your competitors!**

Reason 2: To create a sense of urgency

When would you be more likely to care enough about your health to take action: when your friend suggests you should lose 10 pounds, or when your doctor tells you that if you don't lose 10 pounds, your risk of suffering a heart attack in the next two years increases by 70%?

For all its virtues, the internet still represents "Passive Marketing". In other words, it is a marketing tool that does not require you to do the selling. As with other forms of passive marketing, for people to get excited about your product or service, you need to create that excitement for them.

The next section in the chapter entitled "How do I create a strong call to action?" will provide more details and concrete examples.

Reason 3: Prospects will buy your product or service in a shorter time frame

What if you could create a business where every single prospect you encountered needed your product or service immediately? While this may sound too good to be true, it is possible. The first step is to brainstorm why someone would buy from you instead of your competitors. Take a sheet of blank paper and write down a few reasons.

Did you do it? If you did, good. If not, why not?

Now, take the answers you created above and put some urgency into them. For example, if one of your unique selling points is better pricing, your call to action could be:

> "For only pennies a day, you can have your very own new and improved widget maker! Offer valid while supplies last."

This statement tells your prospects that your product is inexpensive, has recently been upgraded, and that there are a limited number of widget makers available. How many times have you seen this or something similar in a t.v. infomercial?

Reason 4: To convince prospects to buy more of your product/service

In order to convince a prospect to buy more of your product or service, you need to connect with that person on an emotional level. One way to do this is to add emotional ties to your call to action.

For example, "Call today for your chance to win an all-expenses-paid trip to Bermuda!" sends my imagination to work, creating pictures of people sunbathing on the beach, and children building sand castles.

"Call us to win a trip to the beach" is nowhere near as exciting. It lacks the intricate details that create the feeling of relaxation many North Americans associate with beaches, water and free trips across the continent.

How do I Create a Strong Call to Action?

There are 3 easy ways to create a strong call to action:

- create urgency (limited time, limited availability)
- emphasize benefits (lower price, new & improved model available, easy to use)
- solve a prospect's problem (increases revenues, creates more available time, decreases work load, lowers costs)

Create Urgency

Below are a few ways you can create a sense of urgency in your advertising:

- "For only $100, you can own your very own state of the art stereo! Come in and get yours today while supplies last."
- For only three weeks you can come in and get your very own state of the art stereo at rock bottom prices! Come in and get yours today!"

The phrases "while supplies last" and "only three weeks" tell the reader that they need to act quickly if they are contemplating buying your product or service.

Emphasize Benefits

In order for your ideal client to get excited about your product, you need to tell him what problem(s) your product solves. Here are some examples of a primary call to action. See if you can figure out which ones are strong and which ones are weak.

- Give us a call at 416 118 2888.

- Call today for your chance to win a brand new 2006 Jeep Forerunner!

- Come into our store to win.

- Hurry! Don't miss your chance to win a spectacular getaway to the Cayman Islands!

Did you figure it out? If you said that numbers 1 and 3 are weak calls to action and that 2 and 4 are strong, you are right!

Solve a Prospect's Problem

Most North Americans spend money because they have a problem they need resolved. That being the case, which of your ideal visitors' problems can you, your product or your service solve? What follows is a sample call to action form. Fill it out and create a strong call to action for your product or service.

Call to action Component	Write Your Example Here
Feeling of Urgency	
Emphasize Benefits	
Solve a Problem	
Command Attention	
Stir Emotion	

A sample of the above form can be downloaded from www.idealvisitor.com

Chapter Overview

In this chapter you have learned how to:

1. see the message your ideal visitor is receiving

2. identify what your ideal visitor wants to know

3. tell your ideal visitor what he or she wants to know

Coming Up ...

In the next chapter you will learn how to recognize what your ideal visitor wants to do on your website.

CHAPTER 4

▼

WHAT DOES MY WEBSITE NEED TO DO FOR MY IDEAL VISITOR?

What you will learn in this chapter:

1. Why you need to determine what the website *will do* for your ideal visitor

2. How to determine what the website *needs to do* for your ideal visitor

The distinction here is subtle, but important. Most web sites *will do* a lot of things. On the other hand, they probably only *need to do* one or two things, but they need to do them really well. It is important to make certain that your web site *will do* everything it needs to do.

As an example, take a look at the website of any major bank or trust company. Chances are, they have a huge array of on-line features for their customers, ranging from on-line banking and bill payment options, to investments, news and information services, lending products and services, a brief history of interest rates, biographical information about the key corporate personnel, and hundreds more optional services for their internet clients.

Now put yourself into the client's shoes. Chances are you have used the online services provided by your own banking institution. How many of their features do you use? Their web site ***will do*** a lot of things for you, but as an average consumer, you only really ***need it to do*** a handful of different tasks.

Why you need to determine what the web site will do for your ideal visitor

Most North Americans today are looking for easy, inexpensive solutions to the problems they are currently facing.

Very few North Americans spend money unless they are emotionally moved.

You have less than 10 seconds to capture the attention of your ideal visitor before he or she moves on to another potential solution.

This presents three significant challenges for anyone attempting to market their products or services via the internet. Tie the three statements above to the question of what your website will do for your ideal visitor. Your website ***must***

- Present an easy, inexpensive solution to a problem
- Emotionally move each and every prospective customer
- Accomplish both of the above points in ten seconds or less

Faced with this, determining what your website will do is relatively easy, but how to accomplish it is a challenge. Take a minute and think about the problems you face every day in your family and your work. What do you do to resolve the problems? Do you talk about them? Do you take action and seek solutions? What types of solutions do you look for?

There are four basic problems that North Americans are consistently facing in the modern environment:

- Not enough time to do or accomplish everything they want to do

- Not enough money to do or accomplish everything they want to do

- Concerns about health issues

- Concerns about self-esteem issues

While there are a multitude of variations on a theme, most problems or challenges faced by North American consumers today is a subset of one of these four basic types.

Now put on your ideal visitors' hat. Your challenge is to determine what your ideal visitors' problems are, so that you can position yourself as the provider of solutions. Take some time and a fresh sheet of paper. Try to brainstorm what you think their problems are. After you have done this, something to consider is how similar your problems are to those of your ideal visitor. Take some time to run through this exercise carefully. The answers you come up with may surprise you, and more importantly may lead you to a greater understanding of your prospective customers.

The next step is relatively straightforward. After identifying what potential problems your prospective clients are facing, you need to figure out how your product or service can provide a solution. This is not something that anyone else can answer for you. The answers will be different for everyone's products and services, depending on who their ideal client is. On the same sheet of paper, beside each of the possible problems you have identified for your ideal client, write down several ways in which your products or services can provide a solution.

You are now well on your way to reaching your ideal visitor!

Now that you have figured out what types of problems your product or service can resolve, you are ready to figure out what your website needs to do in order to get your ideal visitor to become an ideal client.

How to determine what the website needs to do for your Ideal Visitor

It's great to have a website, but what good is it if it doesn't solve the problems your ideal visitor is facing?

If your ideal visitor is someone who is about to have his or her first child, then they will probably need to purchase:

- Furniture items (crib, changing table, bassinet, etc.)
- things to decorate the bedroom
- toys
- clothes
- diapers and hygiene products
- formula

Put yourself back into your ideal visitor's shoes again for a minute. If this is you, then naturally, you would go to stores that sell products for newborn babies, right? This is just common sense, and works very effectively if you are browsing through a large shopping mall.

When it comes to creating websites, however, that 'common sense' isn't quite so common. People forget to pinpoint the one thing they want their ideal visitors to do (their primary call to action!). Very soon the website becomes a hodge-podge of stuff. Product catalogs, testimonials, articles, etc. all get posted to the website. Largely because the storage space on the web is not physical space, many people tend to fill it up with large quantities of material that distracts from the real purpose they got the website in the first place. The readers get confused, have little time or patience to figure out what the message is, and then go somewhere else to get their problem solved!

Let's go back to the example of the baby's room for a minute. If you want to buy baby's furniture from a website, you would first look for the website of a store that you know sells baby furniture. Once you found the website you would search for the pieces of furniture you need: crib, bassinet, change table, shelves/drawers, etc. To do this, you need a search box and button on the website, and a search function that shows all the products and related information (price, description, picture, etc.) about the products you searched for.

Now it's time to put your own shoes back on for a minute. If you are selling products or services over the internet, your ideal visitor would need to know more than just what items you are selling. You would need to include a description of the items, price, currency (if you are selling out of country), and pictures (if applicable), and any applicable discounts. Even more importantly, you ideal visitor would need to know how to purchase your products (e.g. a link to a step-by-step credit card processor or *Paypal* account) and any delivery details. Finally, you need a mechanism for your visitors to contact you if they have questions, concerns, testimonials or complaints, or simply prefer to deal in person.

Depending upon the nature of your business, you may require a website with a substantial amount of storage space. Pictures, for example, take up a lot more space than text. If you include images or pictures of a lot of your product line, or if you are a photographer and your products **are** pictures, it is important to make sure that your website has the ability to handle the amount of data you intend to load onto it.

This leads to another common error made in setting up websites. Don't assume that everyone visiting your website, including your ideal visitors, have a high speed internet connection. Even in this day and age, many people are still using dial-up connections. They are slower, but they still work just fine. Unfortunately, websites with a lot of graphics content, especially *Flash* files or high resolution photographs, take longer to load. If it takes more than 10 seconds to load your website using a dial-up connection, then you risk losing your customer. How can you avoid this?

- Save the *Flash* presentations for pages further into your website, or set them up so that only visitors who want to delve into them are able to view them.

- Don't put a lot of high resolution photographs on the home page. Instead, use thumbnail size photographs where necessary, that can link to a full-sized photograph if people really want to see it.

Another variation on this theme is to ensure that you design your website to be viewed on even the most basic of monitors. Certain patterned background art, for example, may look great on your computer, and terrible on somebody else's just because their ability to view graphics is more limited (or alternatively, much less limited) than your own.

There is a simple rule of thumb for anyone designing a website anticipating it to be viewed by a large number of people, and in particular prospective customers. Look at it under all circumstances you can think of.

Picture yourself shopping for a new home. You find a place you think is ideal, but it's a nice sunny day and that makes every home look a little bit better. Just to be sure, you come back and visit the same home in the evening. Does the neighbourhood still have the same appeal, or does it look different? What about visiting a third time during a rainstorm? Not only does this give you a chance to see whether the roof leaks, but you can view the neighborhood during a gloomy day.

The same logic applies to a website. You want to see what it looks like on your own computer, but it's worth trying it out on a few others as well. The easiest way to do this is to visit an internet café for an hour or two. View your website on a P.C. and on a Macintosh. See what it looks like using a laptop with an LCD screen as well as a high end desktop monitor.

The long and short of it is simple. You want to view your website, just as you would a prospective home purchase, under the best and worst conditions as well as all point in between.

Now it's time to apply these techniques to your website material. Does your website attract or repel your ideal visitor? If your website repels your ideal visitor, how can you change your information, layout and tools so that it attracts your ideal visitor?

To summarize, you website needs to do the following:

- Provide your prospective customer with the basic information he or she is looking for.
- Issue a primary and secondary call to action
- Provide your customer with a ready means to purchase products or services from you, on line!

- Load onto his computer easily and quickly

- Look appealing under even the most adverse viewing conditions.

Chapter Overview

In this chapter you have learned:

1. why you need to determine what the website will do for your ideal visitor

2. how to determine what the website needs to do for your ideal visitor

Coming Up

In the next chapter you will learn:

1. how to determine what forms of advertising you already have

2. how to determine what you need to create to attract your ideal visitor

CHAPTER 5

▼

WHAT DO I ALREADY HAVE THAT MY IDEAL VISITOR WANTS TO SEE OR KNOW?

What you will learn in this chapter:

1. how to determine what forms of advertising you already have
2. how to determine what you need to create to attract your ideal visitor

How to determine what forms of advertising you already have

This discussion needs to start with a definition of what is meant by "advertising".

Advertising is the "paid promotion of goods, services, companies and ideas by an identified sponsor. Marketers see advertising as part of an overall promotional strategy. Other components of the promotional mix include publicity, public relations, personal selling and sales promotion."

en.wikipedia.org/wiki/Advertising

In order to know what you still need to create or obtain so your ideal client will buy from you (instead of your competition), you need to figure out what you need, and what you have. Again, this sounds like a very simple concept, but it can be very enlightening to discover just what forms of advertising you already have working for you. Many of them can surprise you, as they are not things that you have specifically purchased as advertising, but tend to work for you.

For this chapter, we will utilize the example of someone who is opening a store catering to the golf enthusiast. The store space has already been rented, all the fixtures and equipment have been installed, the business office has been set up and the inventory for sale is already on hand. What is still needed are advertising tools (signs, brochures, business cards, website, etc.)

Below is a list of the more popular types of business advertising, together with a list of some of their advantages and disadvantages. This should not be considered as an exhaustive list, as there are many different types of advertising out there. Likewise, the advantages and disadvantages cited here are general, and should not be considered as a complete list.

Media	Advantages	Disadvantages
Flyer or Brochure	• Inexpensive • Easily created & replicated • Easily distributed	• Can be disposed of easily • Will often be disposed of without being read
Sign	• Expense depends on the size of the sign • Customized to your needs • Unique	• Larger signs are more difficult to handle and take time to create • May require significant expense to set up and maintain
Business Card	• Small • Portable • Inexpensive • Easily copied, distributed and replicated	• Easily filed and forgotten • Can be disposed of easily
Website	• Passive advertising • Simple set up • Expense depends on size and complexity.	• Doesn't necessarily tell people the right message
Radio	• Message gets to a large audience	• Expensive • Smaller conversion rate
Newspaper	• Message gets to a large audience	• Expensive • Smaller conversion rate
Agencies	• Experts handling your need • Assumed larger conversion rates	• Expensive

Media	*Advantages*	*Disadvantages*
Joint Ventures	• 'Win-Win' philosophy is used • Less expensive form of advertising • Allows your tasks to be completed while spending minimal time and money	• Can be challenging to track • Need to make sure both parties hold their side of the agreement

Let's put some of these advertising methods into real scenarios.

Flyers, Brochures & Business Cards

If you're going to a networking event with over 100 people, chances are you're not going to be able to talk to every single person at that event. This is where flyers, brochures and business cards come in handy. Flyers and brochures are great because they are larger than pocket size, so they can stand out from your average business cards, but they are still small enough (or can be folded small enough) for your prospective customer to take back to their office.

Similarly, since business cards are pocket-size, they are easy to carry around and people can take them home after the event. They are great because they can fit into a container for easy reference at a later date, and they will remind your prospects that you can help them.

Signs

Signs can fit into two categories: large and small. The large billboard, window and bench signs obviously are not portable; they must stay where they are. These large signs are great for people to look at when they are driving; the important text is big enough for them to see quickly, and it enables them to keep going. Where are large marketing billboards today? The next time you're on your local freeway, take a look around you. Chances are there are billboards all around: freeway signs, large advertising that you can see from the roadway and animated screen plays at the top of buildings are all examples of signs.

TV, Radio & Newspaper

TV, Radio and the newspaper are great forms of advertising if you want to get your message to a large audience in a short period of time. However, there are some red flags to watch for when using these larger forms of media. The first red flag to watch for is price. Of the three, newspaper is the least expensive; however, if your advertisement is written poorly or placed in a section people won't see, your ad becomes useless. TV and radio get your point across to many people in a short time, but measuring the conversion ratio (how many prospects turn into customers) can be tricky, and these forms of media are very expensive (typically thousands of dollars for a certain number of ad space).

Website

A website brings together the wide audience-base of TV, radio & newspaper, for the relatively inexpensive brochure and business card pricing. Websites today can do so much more than your average paper brochure. You can interact with a website. You can give feedback, have discussions, purchase products, comment on live presentations, and more.

Agencies

Marketing and advertising agencies have the expertise needed to format your material in such a way that it will bring in the prospects for you; however, you will pay more for this help than you would to put a simple brochure or business card together.

Joint Ventures

Of all the available forms of marketing out there today, I like joint ventures the best. Joint ventures are basically two parties (individuals or groups) working together to find a 'win-win' scenario.

Detailed examples of each marketing format can be found at my website, www.idealvisitor.com

How to determine what you need to create to attract your Ideal Visitor

To determine what pieces of information you need to attract your ideal visitor, put together the information you gathered from chapters 1–4:

- Ch 1: who is my ideal visitor
- Ch 2: what does my ideal visitor want to know

- Ch 3: what does my ideal visitor want to do on my website
- Ch 4: what does my website need to do for my ideal visitor

In the space below, write down any notes you have gathered from reading chapters one through four:

Now take a look at the compilation of results you have gathered so far. To demonstrate, I'll use the example of a house being built. When a builder approaches a client, one of the first questions they ask the buyer is "who will live in the house?" It may be two new parents expecting to have three children across the next five years. It may be a family of six with the eldest two children ready to leave for University. It may even be two newly retired grandparents wanting a place to go and relax.

Once you have determined who your ideal visitor is, put yourself in your ideal visitor's shoes. Ask questions like:

- What does my ideal visitor spend his/her time doing?
- What are the main problems and challenges my ideal visitor spends time solving?
- What problem does my website solve?

As you put yourself into the shoes of your ideal visitor, you will discover what he or she wants to know from your website. For example, if you sell babies' shoes, you want to target young mothers. 'Okay, so how do I find young mothers to market to?' Look for developing neighborhoods with daycare and community centers. Put up posters and leave flyers in those neighborhoods.

For more information on choosing the marketing method that best fits your needs, go to www.idealvisitor.com.

Chapter Overview

In this chapter, we have covered:

1. how to determine what forms of advertising you already have

2. how to determine what you need to create to attract your ideal visi-
    tor

CHAPTER 6

▼

WHAT DO I NEED SO I CAN TELL MY IDEAL VISITOR WHAT HE WANTS TO KNOW?

What you will learn in this chapter

1. What a needs analysis is

2. How to do a needs analysis in preparation for your website

3. Necessary parts of an effective website

   a. Website basics

   b. Text (information & call to action)

   c. Pictures/Illustrations

   d. Styles/Layouts/Design

What is a Needs Analysis?

A needs analysis is a set of questions that determines what you have and what you need in order to put together a website for your ideal visitor. Completing a needs analysis can be a straightforward or even sub-conscious task, or a complex process. It all depends on the level of depth and detail you wish to explore.

The human brain completes sub-conscious and un-conscious needs analyses all the time. You instinctively reach for a glass of water when your brain has completed a needs analysis and determined that you are thirsty. Are you aware of all the steps leading to the conclusion that you need to drink a glass of water? Of course not, but your brain has completed them all in logical sequence.

A similar, but more conscious example of a needs analysis would take place in a restaurant. A subconscious analysis has already told you that you are hungry and should eat, and has probably directed you towards a particular type of restaurant. Now you are looking at the menu. What items catch your attention, and why? Different combinations of flavors? Price?

How do I do a Needs Analysis?

When you put together a needs analysis for your website, you need to consider the following questions:

1. Who is your audience/ideal visitor?

2. What do you want your ideal visitor to know?

3. What do you want your ideal visitor to do when they are visiting your website?

Look back to chapters one through three for the answers to these questions. If you have read through these chapters step by step, you have already identified who your ideal visitor is, what they want to know, and what they want to do when they are visiting your website.

Your call to action is what drives people to do what you want them to do (read information, buy product, join a club/association, etc.) What is your call to action? Does it drive people to do what you want them to do? Write down your call to action and read it four or five times out loud. Do you find it compels you to take action (e.g. contact you, buy your product, etc.)? If not, how would you change it so that it compels you to take action?

Necessary Parts of an Effective Website

Website Basics

Before you can begin to build a website, you need to have two things. Although this may sound basic to some, the first step is to secure rights to a unique domain name or *universal resources location* [u.r.l.]. This is your website address and typically begins with www.

The second essential requirement is to arrange for *hosting* services. This is usually done by contract with a third-party supplier. This supplier stores the files that make up your website. Remember, it does not matter where the files are physically located, so long as they are connected to the *World Wide Web*.

To actually create a website requires that certain components be assembled into a cohesive structure. These components include:

- Text/Information content
- Pictures/Images/Illustrations
- Style/Layout/Design

Assembling these components is something that you can do yourself, though it may be time consuming if you are not experienced. You might prefer to contract the services of one or more professionals to assist you. In particular, you may want to investigate the services of:

- A professional copy-writer (someone who can take what you want to say and put it into the right words, both eloquently and quickly)
- A graphic designer (someone who can create a unique style or design custom made for you.)
- A programmer (someone who can translate all of the individual components into the right computer language (s) that work on the world

wide web. In most situations, this would be the "lead hand" or project team co-ordinator.

Text/Information

When you sit down to write the text portion of your website, there are a few questions to consider:

- What does your ideal visitor need to know to solve his problem?

- What does your ideal visitor need to do to solve his problem?

- What information and tools can you supply to help solve his problem?

For example, if someone is looking to buy a book about do-it-yourself home repairs, she would need to know:

- Where to buy the book (website, store, etc.)

- What books are available in a do-it-yourself format on the topic of home repairs

- What the book she chose costs

- Any applicable delivery procedures and costs

- Applicable taxes

- How long she has to wait for delivery

The key to the text messages on your website are to be efficient, yet informative. In terms of content, recognize that most readers today tend to skim, and **will not stop to read the whole content, unless it catches their attention in the first ten seconds or so**. This means that your text has to have *impact*.

In terms of appearance, your text can take on a wide range of type-faces, sizes, styles and colors. While this can serve to ensure that a certain component of your text stands out, don't let the information get lost in the delivery.

Pictures/Images/Illustrations

This essentially includes everything that is not text. You might include a photograph of your product, or your store; diagrams of what your products look like when assembled, or even charts showing the value of your product versus that of your competitor. The category is very broad in scope.

When you are determining what illustrations to add to your website, and where to put them, there are a couple of questions you want to ask yourself:

- Do your photos and illustrations enhance the point of your website and encourage your ideal visitor to complete the call to action?

- Are your illustrations linked to the topic you are talking about?

- If not, what illustrations can you use to further encourage your ideal visitor to take the calls to action?

For example, if you have a company that does chimney sweeping, does your website have pictures of chimneys, chimney sweepers, and all of the appropriate tools used?

The internet is a visual medium, and the effective use of illustrations cannot be understated. At the same time, however, remember that high resolution images can be slow to load onto a customer's computer, and you want to be selective. If you have a lot of images, such as pictures of a whole line of products, then perhaps you want to consider using thumbnail images or even a link to product images on a separate page, rather than forcing the potential customer to wait while hundreds of images are loaded. You want to make certain that the images you select are striking and catch the prospective customer's attention, but do not distract him or her from the actual message of your website. Don't let the pictures overwhelm the call to action.

Styles/Layouts

When you are ready to decide what your website looks like, you can ask yourself a few questions to help you decide on a style and layout:

- What styles (layouts, colors, patterns, fonts, etc.) does your ideal visitor like? For example, if you are an on-line retailer of baby products, chances are that you will use a lot of pinks and blues in your design.

- What type of layout (where the information, pictures, links and buttons are placed) makes navigating your website easiest for your ideal visitor?

- Are there colors, designs or styles your ideal visitor likes? Dislikes? If your ideal customer is of Asian background, extensive use of the color red will have a completely different effect than if your ideal customer is someone seeking assistance with their investment portfolio.

- What styles are used on other websites that your ideal visitor would like? You don't want your website to look like a clone of your competitor's, but at the same time recognize what works and what doesn't. Take advantage of what works.

Chapter Overview

In this chapter, we have covered:

1. What a needs analysis is

2. How to do a needs analysis in preparation for your website

3. Necessary parts of an effective website

    a. Website Basics

    b. text/information & call to action

    c. pictures

    d. styles/layouts

CHAPTER 7

▼

HOW DO I CREATE WHAT MY IDEAL VISITOR WANTS TO SEE?

What you will learn in this chapter:

1. Three different methods of creating websites
2. Determining your strengths and weaknesses (and why this is necessary)
3. How to determine which method best suits:
    a. your capabilities
    b. your ideal visitors' needs

Three Different Methods of Creating Websites

There are three general methods of creating the website for your ideal visitor:

- template
- content management system (aka CMS)

- custom design

Templates

Pros	*Cons*
• Inexpensive	• Restricted to existing design
• Design already exists	• Lacking creativity
• Don't need to know web programming	

Templates are great if you want to put a website together and have little money and expertise around website development. As well, they are an ideal tool for a website where the content is unlikely to experience any significant changes over time. More and more companies today are putting together services that allow the novice website user to build his/her website.

As great as that is, there are some down sides to using a template to create your website. Almost every person I have dealt with who wanted a template to put together their website, has ended up re-creating their website a short way down their business journey. One client I had insisted I use a particular template. I agreed, but throughout the project, warned him of the restrictions he would come across: the existing pages would have to keep the same themes, it would be a lot of work to add new pages to the design, etc. In spite of the warnings I gave, he insisted on using this template. So, we started putting the content into the site.

Less than halfway through the project, he was demanding that all kinds of little things be changed to suit his needs (the color of the text, the positioning of pictures, etc.) I reiterated (yet again) to him that these were restrictions of the template, and would be difficult and costly to change. He made his decisions based on his limited knowledge, and we completed the project.

Less than two months after the project completion, he decided to start a new re-design project because he had lost interest in this particular design and realized its limitations.

The moral of the story: if you want to use a template system, be sure it does what you need now, six months from now, and 6 years from now!

Content Management Systems

Pros	*Cons*
• Inexpensive • Some existing designs to choose from • Ability to create and include your own design • Don't need to know web programming • Easy to update the material in your website	• Restricted to functions the system can provide • Usually need to switch hosting companies

In order to choose a content management system (CMS), you first need to understand a little bit about what the different CMS's can do and what you need it to do.

In order to figure out what you need the CMS to do for you, ask yourself these questions:

- Do you have a design/layout already created?
- Do you know how you want the text laid out?
- Do you have a specific color scheme in mind?
- Do you need flexibility to use HTML tags?
- Do you have lots of links and files you need uploaded?
- Do you need to use third party software (e.g. credit card processing, radio broadcasting, etc.)?

Once you know what you need the CMS to do, there are a few more questions to ask when deciding which CMS service to use:

- What does it cost?

- Is hosting included in the price?

- Is the price monthly or annually?

- How easy is it to learn how to use the system?

- How do you upload pictures? What is the maximum size the picture files can be?

- How do you attach files?

- Can you add page enhancements using buttons? Using HTML? How?

- Is there a limit to the number of links on a page?

- Is there a limit to the size of files (pictures or otherwise)? If so, what is the size limit?

- Are templates included? If so, how many can you choose from?

- Is the system flexible enough for you to create your own design and upload those files?

Custom Design

Pros	Cons
• Crisp clear marketing message conveyed in design • Design is custom-built to your needs • Much more control over site design and functionality	• Expensive • Need to find complimentary services or learn how to put your own site together (hosting, site construction & maintenance)

Having your website custom built is a learning experience for most people that are unfamiliar with the process of website development. Some of the questions that must be answered are:

- Where do I get my site designed?

- What do I want my site to look like?

- How do I know I'm going to get a good design?
- What do my competitors' websites look like?

Each of these questions and more must be answered during the process of website development. We'll go through each of these four questions, and show you the basics of putting your website together.

Where do I get my site designed?

If you, or someone you trust knows a graphic designer, then that would likely be the first person you contact. Unless you have absolute confidence in this individual, though, you would want to interview at least three or four.

To find a graphic designer, go to your local graphic design association. They will have a list of various professional graphic designers in your area. Contact a few of the designers on the list, and request to meet with them. Ask the following sets of questions:

1. How long have you been working as a graphic designer?
2. What are your credentials in the industry?
3. What type of companies have you done designs for?
   a. Entrepreneurs
   b. Small-medium businesses
   c. Large corporations
   d. Government institutions
   e. Not-for-profit organizations
   f. Other
4. Do you have a portfolio you can show me?
5. Can you refer me to some other websites *currently in use* that you created?
6. Are you working for a company, freelancing or running your own business?

7.   How much are your rates?

   a.   Do you charge by the hour or a flat rate pre-negotiated for the entire project?

   b.   How much do you expect to be paid in advance?

Look for signs of professionalism, courtesy and confidence. Out of the three or four people you interview, choose the one that 'fits' with you the best. Which designer:

- You would get along best with?
- Showed you samples closest to your own needs?
- Is in your price range?
- Proved he or she has the qualifications?

What do I want my site to look like?

When you are ready to decide what you want your website to look like, take a look at what type of websites other people in your industry have created. Are they interactive? What is their call to action? Is it compelling? What colors, layouts and fonts do you see that your ideal visitor would like?

In the section below, make a few notes. Be sure to include the website address (www.somesite.com), what you like about it (layout, color scheme, font, button placement, extra tools, ease of use, etc.) and why you like that particular feature. Once you have your list, you can take that to a designer to help you get your website as close as possible to what your ideal visitor wants.

How do I Know I'm going to get a good Design?

Look for training, experience and professionalism. The better qualified the designer, the higher the chances of finding the designer that will work for you. Look for examples of what you are putting together. For example, if you are in the restaurant industry, look for designers who have experience working with restaurants.

What do my Competitors' Websites Look Like?

Why does this matter? It gives you a starting point. It shows you what others in your industry are putting on their website (pictures, layouts, colors, words, etc.). Here's a quick list of items to look for when evaluating your competitors' websites:

- colors

- fonts

- layouts

- animation

- wording

- pictures

- contact and sign-up forms

Make a list of what you like and dislike. This will give your designer a better idea of what to put together to suit your needs. It is important to note that you are not attempting to plagiarize the content of your competitor's website, nor infringe upon what may be a copyrighted design. Rather, you are trying to get a feel for what works and what doesn't work, what you like and what you dislike, what you would want to emulate, and what you would want nothing to do with.

When doing this, make certain that you select competitors' websites carefully. You undoubtedly have several competitors in the industry. It is important to select the competitor that is in direct competition with you. There may be a competitor in the same industry, but the important question really is "Are they competing for the same *ideal client?*" The Boston Pops and the Boston Bruins are arguably both in the entertainment industry. That doesn't mean that they appeal to the same audience.

Determining your Strengths and Weaknesses

Before you decide which website development method works for you (template, custom or content management system), you need to figure out what your strengths and weaknesses are in the areas of website development.

Ask yourself the following questions:

- Do I find it easy to write content that sells? Do I have training in marketing & sales?

- Do I find it easy to paint a picture from scratch using design software?

- Do I find it easy to construct a website from scratch?

- If one or more of the answers to the above questions is no, what part (s) can I afford to get help with?

If you have no training or strength in any of the three areas, then your best approach may be to have someone put together the website for you. If you are comfortable with part of the process, determine which part of the process you can do. From there, decide which method would fit best with your current scenario (see examples below).

I am:

- comfortable fully constructing the site myself

- comfortable with design, but not code or writing

- comfortable with code, but not design or writing

- comfortable with writing, but not code or design

- comfortable with writing and code, but not design

- comfortable with writing and design, but not code

- comfortable with design and code, but not writing

I have been in the website development industry for 7 years(at the time this book was published), and I have yet to find a client or prospective client that is strong in all areas of website development: design, programming and writing. Usually I find people who are comfortable with one or two of the elements.

As a result, I have outlined which method to use with each of the scenarios above. Keep in mind that you are designing your website to suit your ideal visitor. You need to consider which method would attract and 'sell' your product or service to your ideal visitor.

Template

A template should be used when you are comfortable writing the content, but are not comfortable designing or constructing the website, and are happy with a pre-existing design. Templates without an accompanying content management system require some knowledge of website hosting systems (just enough to log into one and upload files). Note: many templates already exist in today's content management systems.

Content Management System

A content management system should be used when you know you will be writing the content yourself, but are not comfortable designing or constructing the website, and need flexibility in how the website looks. Content management systems should also be used when you want to update the website yourself, and have little or no knowledge of website management tools (*i.e.* HTML editors). Note: many content management systems already have a series of templates available for you to use.

Custom Design

A website should be custom designed when you require a crisp, unique, professional image (e.g. A large corporation) or are not sure where to start with your design, and have money available to put towards a unique design.

Chapter Overview

In this chapter, we have covered:

1. Three different methods of creating websites
2. Determining your strengths and weaknesses (and why this is necessary)
3. How to determine which method best suits:
   a. your capabilities
   b. your ideal visitors' needs

Coming Up

How to use each different type of system to create the best website for your ideal visitor.

PART II

▼

CREATING THE IDEAL WEBSITE FOR MY IDEAL VISITOR

Identifying why you want a website may seem the simplest part of the process. In reality, it is the most difficult. This puzzle has already required you to identify who your ideal client is and, more importantly, attempt to mimic and sympathize with their situation, their wants, needs and desires. To do this properly has, by now, probably required you to think and act in ways that are radically different from anything that you have had to do before.

By contrast, the process of creating the website that you have now envisioned is a relatively straightforward process. For one thing, it is much easier to delegate or contract out the parts of the process that you are unable or uncomfortable to complete yourself. For another, much of the process of creating a website is mechanical, rather than intuitive. Although creativity is certainly a requirement, in order to produce the best visual imagery, the most compelling text, etc., the process of actually building a website is comparatively routine in nature.

▼

Chapter 8

Method 1: Using a Template to Create a Website for My Ideal Visitor

What you will learn in this chapter:

- where to find templates
- how to access a template
- how to edit a template

Where do I find Templates?

There are various places to find website templates today. The simplest way to find templates is to go use Internet Explorer (or any other popular web browser) and go to www.google.com. In the search box, type in 'website template' and click the 'search' button. A list of various websites containing website-templates appears. Click on any of the links in the results list.

If you don't find what you're looking for, add more specific terms to your search. For example, if you are looking for a newsletter template with traditional newspaper styles, then you would type something like "free website template newspaper style" into the search bar.

Google Search Tip:

You can leave the quotes in your search terms or remove them. If you leave the quotes there, Google will search for web pages containing all the words inside the quotation marks *in that exact order*. If you remove the quotes, Google will find all web pages with any of the words you entered. In our example of "free website template newspaper style", Google will find any web pages with the words "free website template newsletter style" all together. When you remove the quotes, Google will find any web pages with a combination of one or more of the words 'free website template newsletter style'; it may find web pages with 'free template', or 'website template' or 'free website template' or 'template style'; there are many combinations of word pairings in this example.

If you narrow your search and still don't find what you're looking for, do a Google search for 'website host' 'template'. Many of the hosting companies today have a selection of templates that you can use.

Free Versus Priced

There are two categories of website templates: free and not-free. Most of the free website templates are sufficient for putting together your own simple website. The drawback to this is, quite simply, you get what you pay for. Most companies that provide free website templates do not offer any kind of service or support. As well, free templates tend to have an "out of the box" or "canned" appearance. This provides anyone surfing to the website with a feeling of *deja-vu*. If your prospective customer thinks he or she has browsed your website already, and is still looking to solve their problem, then the natural conclusion they will have is that your website has already failed to provide them with a solution. The result, naturally, is that they browse away immediately and look somewhere else. Once a prospect has left your website, getting them back is much, much harder than getting them to visit the first time.

For a website that has a unique look and feel you will probably want to look at the templates with a price (check out www.allwebco-templates.com). In all my experience editing website templates, this is the company with the simplest editing setup and the most comprehensive set of instructions for editing and uploading your templates. Using a template with a price does not usually require a large investment of cash. As at the publication date of this manual, a typical range of prices for simple templates would fall between $10—$75 (U.S. Currency). The average price is less than $50. Naturally, for a more complex template with added features and benefits, the price is correspondingly higher.

How do I access my template?

Here is a quick set of instructions on how to get to your template.

1. In Internet Explorer, find the template you want to use (see 'Where do I find templates' section from the previous page).

2. If applicable, make the necessary arrangements to purchase it. This is usually done online either using *Paypal* or a credit card.

3. To download it from the Internet, click on the link or button that says 'download' or 'save'. A popup appears asking where to save the file.

4. Choose a folder to save your template in. Write down the folder name, as you will need to find the template again later. You might want to start a new folder for your website redesign, and give it a name you will remember.

How do I edit my template?

The most readily available program for editing HTML is Microsoft FrontPage (this generally comes with MS Office). There are also a wide range of programs, both free and paid, that you can find. For the purposes of this chapter, it will be assumed that you are using MS FrontPage, however most other programs have all the same basic features and abilities.

Once the download is complete, open the folder containing the template. You'll see a couple of folders: one containing the 'HTML' (or web pages) and one containing the pictures. Open the files in the HTML folder in FrontPage or, in the case of AllWebCo templates, Internet Explorer. Once the file you want to edit is open, start clicking on different parts of the page. You will very quickly see what you can and can not edit.

Every template system is a little different, but there are some generalities of what you can customize in your template. As a general rule of thumb, I tell clients that they can edit any of the words they see, and some of the pictures. Be aware that every template has its own set of restrictions. Many existing pieces of the template can be customized to fit your needs (e.g. text color and sizing can be changed), but it takes a fair bit of knowledge about web page editing. The more advanced your knowledge of web page editing, the more you can change and edit yourself.

The process of editing your website is entirely up to you. After you have determined what you want to edit, and what you are able to edit, the next step is simple. Do it!

Chapter Overview

In this chapter you have learned:

- where to find templates
- how to access a template
- how to edit a template

Coming Up ...

In the next chapter you will learn how to find a set of professionals to help you put your website together.

▼

CHAPTER 9

METHOD 2: GETTING A CUSTOM DESIGNED WEBSITE MADE FOR YOUR IDEAL VISITOR

What you will learn:

- Steps involved in creating custom designed websites
- What a graphic designer is and how to choose one
- What a programmer is and how to choose one

What Steps are involved in creating a custom website?

Once you have gone through the steps in chapters one through seven, you are ready to get to the core of developing a customized website. Here is a quick overview of the steps involved in putting together a custom-built website:

1. Choose a graphic designer

2. Have the website designed

3. Choose a programmer

4. Have the website built for you

5. Decide who will maintain the website

    a. You

    b. your staff/associates

    c. a website company

What is a Graphic Designer?

Before you go out and find a graphic designer, it's generally a good idea to know what a graphic designer is and how to find one. We touched on this subject earlier, but now it is time to explore it in more detail. A graphic designer is a professional who creates pictures to put into professional presentations. For example, a graphic designer creates the look and feel of brochures, business cards, posters and any other marketing pieces used in your business. A graphic designer also uses digital technology to create a website. They are not involved in selecting the text or content, but they have some responsibility for what the content *looks* like. The graphic designer is responsible for the look and feel of your website, the colors and textured patterns that are used, the way in which the text and illustrations are laid out over the background, the incorporation of your personal logo into the website, etc.

How do I Find a Good Graphic Designer?

Graphic designers are found across the world. Chances are that you, or someone else within your organization, or certainly someone that you know well has already developed a relationship with one or more graphic designers. Word of mouth is, as always, the best referral. If someone can tell you of a reputable graphic designer, that's probably the first person you want to interview. If that doesn't provide you with the name and contact information of at least three or four graphic designers, there are certainly other ways to find them. To find a graphic designer located in your area, you can look in a variety of places:

• The Internet

• Local technical or design associations

- Marketing firms
- Printing firms

Take a look in your yellow pages for local website developer or design associations. Call up a couple of associations and tell them you're looking for a professional graphic designer to create a website for you. The helpers at the associations typically know of someone who designs websites and can give you a couple of people to contact.

Once you have the names and phone numbers of a couple of graphic designers, call them and ask to set up individual interviews. In the interview, you want to ask the following questions:

1. How long have you been working as a graphic designer?

2. What are your credentials in the industry?

3. What type of companies have you done designs for?

   a. Entrepreneurs

   b. Small-medium businesses

   c. Large corporations

   d. Government institutions

   e. Not-for-profit organizations

   f. Other

4. Do you have a portfolio you can show me?

5. Can you refer me to some other websites *currently in use* that you created?

6. Are you working for a company, freelancing or running your own business?

7. How much are your rates?

   a. Do you charge by the hour or a flat rate pre-negotiated for the entire project?

   b. How much do you expect to be paid in advance?

To find the best designer for your project, consider how long the designer has been doing graphic design, the types of companies he's been working for, and what his portfolio consists of. Take a look at how he presents himself and his work. Talk about what you like and dislike as you go through the portfolio pieces. Get a feel for how the designer would fit with you: your personality, communication style, preferred design style, industry expertise etc. You want to interview this person as though you were considering hiring him or her for a permanent position at your firm—make certain that he or she is someone that you can work with. There is nothing wrong with interviewing three or four graphic designers, or more.

Once you have chosen a designer, get together with him or her and start discussing your needs for the project. Go through the design process step by step:

- Meet and sign the necessary contracts and agreements. Ensure that the final design becomes your property!

- Advise the designer of your requirements. What you need, what you would like, and what you expect.

- Have the designer create two or three variations of a design built around your needs and wants.

- Review these designs: what do you like about them? What do you want different? Are there elements of the designs that you want put together?

- Have the designer put together a final version of the design.

- When you are satisfied, request a copy of the original design file.

Once you have a copy of the design, you are ready to find a programmer.

What is a programmer?

A programmer is the person who makes the website work and gets it seen by the various search engine programs. Put quite simply, the programmer takes the puzzle pieces created by the graphic designer and the writer, and fits them together for the world to see the finished picture.

Some of the tools a programmer will put together are:

- On-line stores (like amazon.com)

- Newsletters

- 'Static' websites (websites that have no moving or interactive parts)

- Databases

- Animation

- Automatic update features (e.g. date and time)

The programmer is typically proficient in using a variety of different computer languages that are found across the internet. This would include not just simple HTML, but languages such as Java, Flash, C++, and Perl, to name just a few. Although most programmers are proficient with a wide range of languages, they all have their areas of expertise and specialty. To the un-initiated, it can be very difficult to identify a programmers strengths and weaknesses.

How do I find a good programmer?

Again, chances are that you or someone you know already has a strong relationship with a competent programmer. Again, word of mouth is the best place to start, and if someone you trust feels comfortable referring you to someone, then chances are they are capable of meeting your needs. As with graphic designers, however, it never hurts to interview several. You need to be sure that the programmer you select is someone you can work with. This last point is particularly true if you are going to negotiate a long-term contract with them to look after maintaining and updating your website.

If you are not able to find a referral to a programmer, you can use the same techniques that were identified earlier for finding a graphic designer.

When you have created a short list of programmers, companies, locations and contact information (phone, email, fax, other), start contacting some of them and request time to interview each one individually. Tell them where you found their contact information, and what you want help with. Ask to book a time when both of you can sit down and discuss how closely your needs match his/her qualifications. Set aside at least an hour to interview each person.

When you and the programmer sit down together, first go through basic intro-ductions—who you are, what you have done for the last couple of years with respect to your occupation. When basic introductions are complete, get to the meat of the interview; the reason you are getting together. You want to ask the programmer the following questions:

1.how long have you been programming?

2.who have you worked for? (you are looking for a variety of individuals, small companies and larger corporations)

3.what websites have you created? (at this point, request to look at his port-folio)

4.what part(s) of the website(s) did you construct?

Once you have completed the meat of the interview, it is time to find out if they can actually help you. Ask questions like:

1.have you ever created a website like the one I need?

2.(if yes): what did you do? How long did it take?

3.do you charge by the project or by the hour? What are your rates?

To get a sense of how long a particular website should take to build, ask a variety of programmers. You will get varying answers, but they should all be in the same ball-park. For example, if you want a simple six-page website, with text and a few pictures about who you are, what you do and how to contact you for more infor-mation, the prices should all be within $300 of each other. Pay close attention to any quotes that are really high or really low (from the median price), as these may have extras built in that you may not need, or parts left out that you will be billed for at a later date.

From there, choose a quotation. Call the respective programmer and tell him or her of your final decision. Ask the programmer what the next steps are. Look for a request to meet and sign some basic agreements. You may be requested to give the programmer a deposit for service.

From there the project gets underway, and the construction begins. This is the part that you don't have to worry about! The programmer will take the design that the graphic designer has made (see the previous section for how to work with a graphic designer) and connect the pieces, so that the world will be able to see your final product.

Chapter Overview

In this chapter you have learned:

1. Steps involved in creating custom designed websites

2. What a graphic designer is and how to choose one

3. What a programmer is and how to choose one

Coming Up ...

In the next chapter you will learn what a content management system (CMS) is and how to develop a website using a simple CMS.

▼

CHAPTER 10

METHOD 3: BUILDING A WEBSITE USING A CMS SYSTEM

What you will learn in this chapter:

- Where to find a CMS system
- How to access and use a CMS system

Finding a CMS system

Generally, the most effective way to find a CMS system is to contact your host or another provider of hosting services. Most providers also have their own CMS system which they can make available to you. There are several ways in which to locate a provider of CMS systems, including:

- The internet
- Yellow pages
- Referral from other users

Pop culture today provides us with many examples of CMS systems in popular use. The most common today might be "myspace.com" or "facebook.com"

Accessing and utilizing a CMS system

The providers of proprietary CMS systems will provide you with a variety of different standard template designs to use and modify for your own website. Although this is similar to the process of using a template, it is actually quite different. You have fewer options in terms of the types of templates available, however the programming of the website itself is greatly simplified. Most CMS systems will provide you with step-by-step instructions.

PART III

▼

CONNECTING YOUR IDEAL VISITOR WITH YOUR WEBSITE

Now that you have built your website, the next crucial step is making certain that it gets seen by the people who need to see it, namely your ideal clients. This is a step that is often ignored, or poorly performed, but it is in fact just as critical as identifying your ideal clients.

CHAPTER 11

▼

CHOOSING A WEBSITE NAME YOUR IDEAL VISITOR WILL REMEMBER

What you will learn in this chapter:

- what is a url?
- connection between url and website name
- how to choose a website name your ideal visitor will remember
- where to get a website name

What is a URL?

URL stands for "Universal Resource Locator". A URL is the address of a resource on the Internet. In plain English, a URL is the numeric version of a website name.

What is the Connection Between a URL and a Website Name?

Just like every house and apartment in North America has a number identifying its positioning on a street, every website has a numeric address assigned to it. This numeric address tells the website browsers (e.g. Internet Explorer) where in cyberspace to find the desired website. When the website name is chosen, it is told what 'address' to look for, so that it can find and display the correct information for that website name.

For example, a website may have the URL 198.294.356.793 (at the time of writing, this example does not correspond to any existing web page); the corresponding website name may be www.acmewidgetcompany.com. Which combination are you more likely to remember: the twelve digits or the website name? It is for this reason that the earlier versions of Microsoft Internet Explorer switched from numeric addresses to alphanumeric addresses. When the Internet first came out, people had to remember all kinds of combinations of numbers to find a website. As the Internet evolved, the developers created naming systems so people could remember the location of a website with less effort.

How do I Choose a Website Name my Ideal Visitor will Remember?
Associate it with something relevant

If your website is promoting the benefits of a style of baby clothing, would you name your website after a home renovation store? No!
It sounds crazy, but some people do this very thing when choosing a name for their website; they pick a website name that is very long and difficult to remember, or they choose a name that is only a couple of letters and therefore has little or no significance to the material in the website. Worse still, many choose a name that has considerable significance to them, but means nothing to anyone else.

The most popular way North Americans choose a name for their website, is connecting that website name with their company, product or service. That's good if you sell toys and your company name is 'Toys R Us'. What happens if you are starting a new business and have very little client base? What do you use then?

Here are a few things you can think about when you go to choose a website name:

1. What you are selling on the website

2. Your company name

3. The name of a product

For example, if you sell widgets and you want your website to tell your customers where you are and what widgets you sell, you may choose a website name like WidgetWizard.com or Widgetmaker.com. These two website names tell your ideal visitor what you sell, and imply that you are good at what you do.

Don't make it too short or too long

If your website name is too short, you take the risk that people won't be able to associate your website name with your company name, brand, product or service (result: people forget you and your product or service). Why does this matter? Many people in North America today use the power of association to help them remember important information.

When I was in school, I took music lessons. The first thing my music teacher taught us was the names of the notes on the lines and in the spaces. She used association to help us remember the note names. For the names of the notes on the lines, she told us to repeat the following phrase to ourselves: "Every Good Boy Deserves Fudge". Each capital letter starting a new word represented a note on the lines of the music staff.

"Okay, but how does this relate to websites?"

Good question. Let's take another example—www.adt.com. What does ADT stand for? What do they do? What do they sell? Without looking up the actual website (or knowing its brand from TV and radio), it's hard to tell that ADT is a security company. In contrast, if your website name is too long, you run the risk of your clients forgetting it altogether! For example, originally, I used my full company name—Passionate Web Creations—as my website name (www. passionatewebcreations.com). I soon realized that people were having a hard time remembering my website and company name. When I switched it to www.passionateweb.com, people found it easier to remember.

Make it Relevant

If you have a personal website, and your name is Hayley Smith, would you name your website bobdoe.com? No. Why not? Your name is Hayley Smith, not Bob Doe. So, if you sell sports cars—let's say your company is Porsche—would you name your website pip.com? No. Why not? Because your company name is Porsche, not Pip, right?

This sounds like common sense, but people today still use generic names. For example, one day I did a search on 'car parts' (I was looking to replace the windshield of my car) and found the following website name: www.europartsetc.com. All that this particular website name tells me is that the website is about European parts. It doesn't say anything about European parts of what or for what. What is the significance of the 'etc' at the end.… does this mean the company sells parts from regions other than Europe?

In contrast, www.autopartsway.ca gives the viewer a pretty good idea of what he will find on this website: descriptions of auto parts in Canada (and possibly the ability to purchase those parts from the website).

Where do I get a Website Name?

Any website development company offers the option to purchase hosting and a website name. Some of the more popular website name companies in North America are www.godaddy.com and www.domain.com.

Who do I choose for a website name supplier?

This depends on your own criteria:

- who you know (or know of) that sells website names
- whether you want to purchase the hosting from the same place as the website name

- how much you want to pay

Chapter Overview

In this chapter, we have covered:

- What a url is
- The connection between url and website name
- How to choose a website name your ideal visitor will remember
- Where to get a website name

CHAPTER 12

▼

CHOOSING A WEBSITE HOSTING COMPANY

What you will learn in this chapter:

- what is a hosting company
- how hosting companies differ from each other
- where to find hosting companies
- how to identify what you need from a hosting company
- how to purchase a hosting plan

What is a Hosting Company?

A hosting company is essentially a place where you save your web pages so the world can see them. The simplest parallel is a large filing cabinet. The cabinet has drawers and folders with labels on them. A hosting company has one or more computers with lots of space on each computer. The space is divided into 'folders', each having its own 'label' (login name and password). When you look in your 'folder', you see the individual HTML pages and any images or other files that belong on the pages.

How do Hosting Companies Differ from One Another?

Hosting companies are plentiful, and the difficulty is telling one from another. something to bear in mind is that the average person visiting your website will never have any reason to identify which company you have selected to host your website. Here are some key questions to ask the hosting company:

1. Do you have backup servers?

2. Where are your servers located?

3. What happens if there is a power failure?

4. What is the percentage of 'down time' (time when the website cannot be seen online)?

5. What do your hosting packages cost? Is that monthly or annually?

6. How long a contract must I sign?

7. Is there a setup fee?

8. What do your packages include?

    a. How many email addresses do I get?

    b. What type of programming do they support?

    c. How much information can be sent back and forth?

    d. Can I put downloadable files on my website?

Where do I find Hosting Companies?

You can find information on hosting companies on the Internet. Go onto your computer, and open up Internet Explorer (or an equivalent web browser). Open your favorite search engine (Yahoo, Google, etc.). In the search box, type in the phrase: 'web hosting'. If you want to search for a hosting company in a certain area, add that to the end of your search criteria (e.g. 'web hosting' Michigan). It is important to be aware that geography has little or nothing to do with web hosting, other than to satisfy legal requirements. Many companies situated in Canada use a web host that is located in the United States, or Europe. Some jurisdictions outside of North America may require that your host be physically located in the same country as your business. From your own perspective, you want to be certain that your host is reliable and accountable. For this reason, if you are operating a business in California, you may be disinclined to use a host service in Africa. In the event of any problems, you may have little or no legal or financial recourse against the host company.

Returning to the internet search, when you click the 'search' button, the Internet will find all of the websites with the words you typed into the search box. In this case, the search engine will find all the websites with the words 'web hosting' sitting together and any websites with the word Michigan. The websites that match the search terms the closest will be towards the top of the list (usually the very top of the list is taken by sponsored or paid links).

How do I Know what I Need from a Hosting Company?

To determine what services you need from a hosting company, connect with your team of website developers. The designer and the programmer (the person putting the website together for you) can tell you what you need. Some websites require very large amounts of storage space (e.g. large on-line stores, or an internet-based art gallery). Others, such as a basic website with up to 6 pages, each consisting of text and one image, require very little storage space. Some require special interpreters (e.g. databases and Flash movies) and others only need the ability to display HTML.

If you had a website which consisted of large quantities of Flash files, then you would want to be certain the hosting company you have selected provided support for this kind of file, and had a solid reputation for updating themselves regularly as new and enhanced versions of Flash became available.

How do I purchase Hosting? What is Included?

When you find the website host that is right for you, contact them, and ask them about what 'plans' they have to offer. They will provide you with a list of what each hosting plan contains. Your programmer can help you decide what package is right for you, and may even arrange to purchase the hosting on your behalf. If you want to purchase the hosting yourself, you will need to contact the hosting company and provide them with some basic information:

- name

- address

- which hosting package you want

- billing/credit card information

- any email addresses you want to set up

Most hosting provides for several e-mail addresses. Even if your business is a small one-person shop, it can be helpful to have multiple e-mail addresses, just as a means of differentiating what aspect of the business any given e-mail relates to, for example:

- sales@mycompany.com

- service@mycompany.com

- accounting@mycompany.com

- feedback@mycompany.com

- myname@mycompany.com

Every single one of these could be directed to the same person, but should be kept separate simply as a way to keep your business organized. That way, if your business grows to the point that you do hire other people to take on these roles, you don't need to change an established e-mail address.

Chapter Overview

In this chapter you have learned:

- what a hosting company is

- how hosting companies differ from each other

- where to find hosting companies

- how to identify what you need from a hosting company

- how to purchase a hosting plan

CHAPTER 13

▼

TIPS & TRICKS TO HELP YOUR IDEAL VISITOR FIND YOUR WEBSITE

What you will learn in this chapter:

- search engine submission tips
- how to link to other meaningful websites
- how to use keywords & descriptions

Search Engine Submission Tips

There are two types of search engine submission: manual and automatic. We will go through the process of each type in detail. To help your website move up the ranks closer to the first page of links, you should submit your website name once every month. You can do this manually or automatically.

Manual Search Engine Submission

To submit your website to the search engines manually, you need to first open each search engine's web page individually (e.g. Google, Yahoo, etc.) For illustration purposes, we will use www.google.com to explain the submission process.

First, open www.google.com/addurl/ in the web browser of your choice. Once the web page is open, locate the 'URL' and 'comments' boxes. In the 'URL' box, enter the name of your website (www.websitename.com). In the comments box, type a basic description of your website. Next, enter the letters in the box (letters are squiggly) and click the 'submit' button. Once you press the submit button, you will see a screen with a message confirming that you have submitted your website.

Complete this procedure for each search engine you wish to submit your website to.

Automatic Search Engine Submission

Automatic search engine submission requires a piece of software. Each piece of software works a little bit differently, but for the purposes of this illustration we will assume you are using a simple piece of freeware (free downloadable software).

First, you need to download or install your chosen search engine submission tool. For free search engine submission software, go to http://www.download.com/; in the search box, enter 'search engine submission'. Choose a piece of software to download. Once you have chosen what to download, click the link for that software, and follow the installation instructions (most installations are simple to complete).

Once the software is installed, find the area of the screen where you enter the website name, and enter it. Next, find the area of the software that tells you which search engines your website is to be submitted to. This page usually gives you the option to include or exclude any of the search engines or directories listed. Once you have selected which search engines or directories to submit your website to, press the 'submit' button (or an equivalent button). The software will go through each search engine and automatically submit your website, including all sub-pages.

The advantage to using such a piece of software and submitting your website automatically is, quite simply, speed. It does the job quickly and with little or no participation from you.

Using the Keyword and Description Meta Tags

Although the keyword and description meta tags are rarely used these days, a brief description of what they are and how to use them is appropriate.

Meta tags are special instructions that help search engines find your website. Two special meta tags are the "keyword" and "description" tag. The "keyword" tag lists various words you would type into Google (or some other search engine or directory) to find your website. For example, to find a website selling widgets, in the Google search box you would enter something like 'buy widgets'. The phrase 'buy widgets' is one example of a keyword. The sentences you see below each link that is listed in the results are collectively called the description.

This book does not cover the exact HTML to create meta tags. For instructions on how to create meta tags, enter 'meta tag creation' in your chosen search engine. Choose one of the links and follow the directions on the chosen page.

Using Keywords in Content

This is a much more widely accepted principle in search engine submission today. This involves figuring out your keywords ahead of time and including them various times within the content of each web page (especially in headings and summaries). For example, if you have a paragraph about dogs and what breeds are considered smartest in North America, you would include words like 'dogs', 'breeds', 'smartest', and 'North America' as many times as grammatically possible within your material and section titles.

How to Link to Other Meaningful Websites

In order to figure out how to link to other meaningful websites, we first need to define a 'meaningful website'. A meaningful website is a website that is connected in some way to your website. For example, if your website showcases your photography and advertises your photography services, some meaningful websites would be other photographers, photo printing facilities and tools (printers, paper, etc.). In contrast, a website that is meaningless to a photographer's services would contain information about how to breed dogs and applicable area laws and bylaws.

In order to link to other 'meaningful' websites, simply enter the HTML to make a link (for full details see http://www.w3.org/TR/html4/struct/ links.html#h-12.1) into the HTML of your web page.

For someone else to add your link to their websites (e.g. on an affiliates or associates page) email that person and ask if they are willing to list your website on their website. If they agree, send that person the link to your website (e.g. www.mysite.com). Typically, adding a website link is a mutual task. If you ask someone to add a link to your site onto their page, you return the favor by listing their website on your links page. Examples of associates you can exchange links with are: family, friends, and business associates (distributors, customers, suppliers, service providers, etc.)

Chapter Overview

In this chapter you have learned:

- search engine submission tips
- how to link to other meaningful websites
- how to use keyword and description tags

Chapter 14

▼

Bringing it all together.

What you have already learned:

- How to identify your ideal client
- How to create the ideal website to suit your needs
- How to connect your website with your ideal client

The internet can be one of the most powerful tools to help you market your products and services. A well-designed website will help you distribute information and grow your sales revenues. Just as easily, though, a poorly made web presence can accomplish nothing, or worse, work against you. The most important skill is being able to tell the difference. Build onto your good websites, and reconstruct the ones that are not performing for you.

Words of wisdom

This book is meant as a guide; a reference to help you build your business, and steer a course towards success. It must be remembered, however, that not everyone is in a position to take care of everything. This guidebook has given a great many tips for how to contract out or delegate some of the mechanical aspects of creating a website. Equally, it is possible to contract out some of the research necessary to complete part one of this book. ***If you are not in a position to do the job well yourself, don't sacrifice your business by doing the job half-way. Better to hire someone else that can do the job well.***

The last step of building any website should always be ***continual review and upgrade***. What works perfectly today may not be suitable tomorrow. Building a great new website is a fantastic business advantage, but if you competitor builds an identical site, or even worse a better site, then he or she has upped the ante. Just as you need to be competitive in your core business, you also need to have a competitive website. Keep an eye on what the competition is doing, and try to stay ahead of them. Watch out for new competitors entering the market, and for new market niches to open in the future. Modify your website accordingly. ***A good website is a process, not an event.***

References

1. Klemmer, Brian; If how-to's were enough, we'd all be rich, skinny and happy

About the Author

Alison Silbert was born and raised in Mississauga, Ontario. Stricken with epilepsy from a young age, she has persevered and gradually overcome this debilitating condition. She graduated from Humber College in August of 2000 with a diploma in computer programming. Since then, her career has involved large institutions as well as small businesses. Coming from a family with a strong history of entrepreneurship, it was only natural that she developed her own website development company in 2003. This company was built around the single premise that a significant part of the business community had the un-met need of learning how to reach their ideal clients via the Internet. Alison has had a lifelong involvement in the educational environment, and it was only natural that she developed a strong desire to teach and pass on her skills and expertise to others in need. As such, her company has grown, diversified, and taken on a range of associates in different professions. She still lives in Mississauga with her husband, her infant son, and a very loyal Sheltie named Cocoa.

978-0-595-47089-1
0-595-47089-0

www.ingramcontent.com/pod-product-compliance
Lightning Source LLC
Chambersburg PA
CBHW051256050326
40689CB00007B/1216